Chocolate

Chocolate

Delicious recipes from candies to cakes

Love Food ® is an imprint of Parragon Books Ltd

Parragon
Queen Street House
4 Queen Street
Bath BA1 1HE, UK

ISBN: 978-1-4075-3965-2

Printed in China

Internal design by Fiona Roberts
Photography by Mike Cooper
Food styling by Sumi Glass and Lincoln Jefferson
Introduction text by Linda Doeser

NOTES FOR THE READER

This book uses imperial, metric, and US cup measurements. Follow the same units of measurement
throughout; do not mix imperial and metric. All spoon measurements are level: teaspoons are
assumed to be 5 ml, and tablespoons are assumed to be 15 ml. Unless otherwise stated, milk
is assumed to be whole, eggs and individual vegetables such as potatoes are medium, and
pepper is freshly ground black pepper.

The times given are an approximate guide only. Preparation times differ according to the techniques
used by different people and the cooking times may also vary from those given as a result of the
type of oven used. Optional ingredients, variations or serving suggestions have not been included
in the calculations.

Recipes using raw or very lightly cooked eggs should be avoided by infants, the elderly, pregnant
women, convalescents, and anyone with a chronic condition. Pregnant and breastfeeding women are
advised to avoid eating peanuts and peanut products. Sufferers from nut allergies should be aware
that some of the ready-prepared ingredients used in the recipes in this book may contain nuts.
Always check the packaging before use.

Contents

Introduction 06

Heavenly Chocolate 10

Coffee-Time Treats 30

Crumbly Chocolate 52

Delectable Desserts 74

Index 96

Introduction

"Blissful," "heavenly," "divine," or even "to die for"—words of praise we immediately associate with this magical foodstuff. However, chocoholics of the twenty-first century are far from the first people to regard this unique, indulgent treat as precious and associate it with paradise. In the eighteenth century, the Swedish botanist Carolus Linnaeus, who devised a scientific system for classifying plants, named the cacao bush from which chocolate is produced *Theobroma*—food of the gods. But cocoa beans were also highly valued by the native people of Central and South America centuries before any European landed on its shores.

The Mayan people not only ate the sun-dried beans, probably ground to a paste and possibly mixed with water, but cultivated the bushes on which they grew. Depictions of the god *Ek-chuah* processing cocoa still exist today and it is also known that the Mayan people used the beans as a form of currency for trade before their civilization severely declined around 900 AD. Farther north in what is now Mexico, the Toltec people also valued the sun-dried beans and when they were conquered by the Aztecs in 1325, cocoa beans became the currency of the new empire.

The World's Favorite Confectionery

The chocolate of today is very different from that of pre-Columbian America. The Aztecs had discovered that if the beans fermented before they dried in the sun, they had a less bitter flavor, and they also developed techniques for crushing, roasting, grinding, and mixing the fat-rich cocoa paste with cold water. Chocolate was now a drink, served to kings and princes in gold cups.

In the sixteenth century, the Spanish conquistadors began to flavor the drink with spices from Spain and regarded it as a stimulant that improved the endurance of soldiers. It then became fashionable in Spain itself and its Caribbean colonies, but nowhere else, until the Italians became aware of it 100 years later and began to import cocoa beans. From there the fame of this now hot rather than cold drink, sometimes made with milk, spread throughout Europe. Fashionable chocolate houses appeared in all the major cities from Vienna to London and poems were written in praise of this elixir.

The transformation from drink to confectionery could not begin until the dawn of the Machine Age. Separating out the cocoa butter was the first stage in 1828, patented by Dutchman C. J. van Houten, and other developments followed, but it was Swiss confectioners who produced the first real "eating" chocolate.

Types of Chocolate

The quality of chocolate depends on the quality of the raw ingredients and on the manufacturing process. As a general rule, the higher the percentage of cocoa butter, the better the flavor and texture of the product—and the higher the price. Good chocolate should be even in texture with no grains or specks and should have a distinctive chocolate taste rather than a flavor of cocoa. It should melt on the tongue and not feel sticky or greasy. With the exception of couverture (see below), all types of chocolate are made in varying quality.

* Milk chocolate has added milk solids, usually about 14 percent, and milk fats. It is quite sweet with up to 55 percent sugar. It is light brown in color.

* Semisweet chocolate is dark brown and only lightly sweetened.

* Bittersweet chocolate is very dark, sometimes almost black, and is very lightly sweetened.

* Couverture is always high-quality semisweet or bittersweet chocolate designed for cooking, frosting, and making confectionery. It has a high percentage of cocoa butter, which makes it very workable, but it must be tempered before use. This involves heating and cooling to specified temperatures and then working the chocolate with a metal spatula.

* White chocolate is not strictly chocolate because it is made from cocoa butter but contains no cocoa solids. It is more accurately known as white confectionery coating, but you are unlikely to see it advertised in this way on supermarket shelves.

* Chocolate glacé has a high proportion of vegetable fat and is low in cocoa butter. It melts easily and is low in price, but the flavor is poor and it is not recommended for the recipes in this book.

* Cocoa powder is usually unsweetened and is widely used in baking. Drinking chocolate is not a substitute because it has a much milder flavor and contains sugar.

Heavenly Chocolate

Chocolate Fudge Cake

SERVES 8

To make the frosting, put the chocolate, sugar, butter, evaporated milk, and vanilla extract in a heavy-bottom saucepan. Heat gently, stirring constantly, until melted. Pour into a bowl and let cool. Cover with plastic wrap and let chill for 1 hour, or until spreadable. Preheat the oven to 350°F/180°C. Grease and line two 8-inch/20-cm cake pans with parchment paper.

To make the cake, put the butter and sugar in a bowl and beat until light and fluffy. Gradually beat in the eggs. Stir in the corn syrup and ground almonds. Sift the flour, salt, and unsweetened cocoa into a bowl, then fold it into the cake batter. Add a little water if necessary to make a dropping consistency. Spoon the cake batter into the prepared pans and bake in the preheated oven for 30–35 minutes, until springy to the touch and a skewer inserted into the center comes out clean.

Let the pans stand for 5 minutes, then turn out the cakes onto wire racks to cool. When the cakes are completely cooled, sandwich them together with half of the frosting. Spread the remaining frosting over the top and sides of the cake, swirling it to give a frosted appearance.

$\frac{3}{4}$ cup unsalted butter, softened, plus extra for greasing

scant 1 cup superfine sugar

3 eggs, beaten

3 tbsp corn syrup

3 tbsp ground almonds

$1\frac{1}{2}$ cups self-rising flour

pinch of salt

$\frac{1}{3}$ cup unsweetened cocoa

FROSTING

8 oz/225 g semisweet chocolate, broken into pieces

$\frac{1}{2}$ cup dark brown sugar

1 cup unsalted butter, diced

5 tbsp evaporated milk

$\frac{1}{2}$ tsp vanilla extract

Chocolate Truffle Torte

SERVES 10

Preheat the oven to 425°F/220°C. Grease and line a 9-inch/23-cm springform cake pan with parchment paper. Put the sugar and eggs in a heatproof bowl set over a saucepan of gently simmering water. Whisk together until pale and resembling the texture of mousse. Sift in the flour and unsweetened cocoa and fold gently into the batter. Pour into the prepared pan and bake in the oven for 7–10 minutes, or until risen and firm to the touch.

Take the cake out of the pan and place on a wire rack to cool. Wash and dry the pan and replace the cooled cake in the pan. Mix together the coffee and cognac and brush over the cake. To make the truffle filling, put the cream in a bowl and whisk until just holding very soft peaks. Put the chocolate in a heatproof bowl set over a saucepan of gently simmering water until melted. Let cool. Carefully fold the cooled melted chocolate into the cream. Pour the chocolate mixture over the sponge. Chill until set.

To decorate the torte, sift unsweetened cocoa over the top and remove carefully from the pan. Using strips of card or waxed paper, sift bands of confectioners' sugar over the torte to create a striped pattern. Cut into slices with a hot knife to serve.

SPONGE
unsalted butter, for greasing
1/4 cup superfine sugar
2 eggs
1/4 cup all-purpose flour
1/4 cup unsweetened cocoa
4 tbsp cold, strong black coffee
2 tbsp cognac

TRUFFLE FILLING
2 1/2 cups whipping cream
15 oz/425 g semisweet chocolate,
  broken into pieces

TO DECORATE
unsweetened cocoa
confectioners' sugar

Marble Cake

SERVES 10

Preheat the oven to 350°F/180°C. Grease a 6-cup/1.7-liter ring mold. Put the chocolate and coffee in a heatproof bowl set over a saucepan of gently simmering water. Heat until melted. Let cool. Sift the flour and baking powder into a bowl. Add the butter, sugar, eggs, ground almonds, and milk. Beat well until smooth.

Transfer half of the batter to another bowl and stir in the vanilla extract. Stir the cooled soft chocolate into the other half of the batter. Place spoonfuls of the 2 batters alternately into the ring mold, then drag a skewer through to create a marbled effect. Smooth the top. Bake in the preheated oven for 50–60 minutes, until risen and a skewer inserted into the center comes out clean. Leave in the mold for 5 minutes, then turn out onto a wire rack to cool.

To make the frosting, put the chocolate, butter, and water in a heatproof bowl set over a saucepan of simmering water. Heat until melted. Stir and pour over the cake, working quickly to coat the top and sides. Let set before serving.

1 cup unsalted butter, softened,
  plus extra for greasing
2 oz/55 g semisweet chocolate
1 tbsp strong black coffee
2 cups self-rising flour
1 tsp baking powder
1 cup superfine sugar
4 eggs, beaten
$1/2$ cup ground almonds
2 tbsp milk
1 tsp vanilla extract

FROSTING
$4^1/_2$ oz/125 g semisweet
  chocolate
2 tbsp unsalted butter
2 tbsp water

Rippled Chocolate Gâteau

SERVES 10

Preheat the oven to 375°F/190°C. Oil and line two 7-inch/18-cm shallow cake pans with parchment paper. Cream together the butter, sugar, and vanilla extract until light and fluffy. Stir in the eggs one at a time, adding a little flour after each addition. When all the eggs have been added, stir in the remaining flour and the ground almonds. Add 1–2 tablespoons of cooled boiled water and mix lightly to form a smooth dropping consistency.

Melt the 1 oz/25 g of chocolate in a heatproof bowl set over a saucepan of gently simmering water. Stir until smooth, then pour over the cake batter and gently mix in a figure-eight action. Take care not to over-mix or the rippled effect will be lost. Divide between the 2 cake pans and smooth the tops. Tap them lightly on the counter to remove any air bubbles.

Bake in the preheated oven for 25–30 minutes or until golden and the tops spring back when touched lightly with a finger. Remove from the oven and leave for 10 minutes before transferring to a wire rack and discarding the parchment paper. Let stand until cold before frosting.

To make the frosting, break the chocolate into small pieces and place in a heavy-bottom saucepan. Add the butter and maple syrup. Heat gently, stirring frequently, until the chocolate has melted and the mixture is smooth. Add the sugar and stir gently until the mixture is well blended. Let stand until cool and beginning to thicken. Beat occasionally during this time.

Split each cake in half and use one-third of the cooled frosting to sandwich the 4 layers together. Spread an additional third around the sides of the cake and roll in the toasted slivered almonds. Spoon the remaining frosting on top and spread with a swirling action to give a decorative effect. Sprinkle with the chocolate shavings and serve.

1 tsp sunflower oil, for oiling
3/4 cup unsalted butter or margarine, softened
1 1/2 cups superfine sugar
1 tsp vanilla extract
3 eggs, beaten
1 cup self-rising flour
1/4 cup ground almonds
1–2 tbsp cooled boiled water
1 oz/25 g semisweet chocolate

FROSTING
8 oz/225 g semisweet chocolate, broken into pieces
5 tbsp unsalted butter
2 tbsp maple syrup or corn syrup
1/2 cup dark brown sugar

TO DECORATE
1/4 cup slivered almonds, toasted
chocolate shavings

Mocha Layer Cake

SERVES 8

Preheat the oven to 350°F/180°C. Lightly grease three 7-inch/18-cm layer cake pans.

Sift the flour, baking powder, and unsweetened cocoa into a large mixing bowl. Stir in the sugar. Make a well in the center and stir in the eggs, corn syrup, oil, and milk. Beat with a wooden spoon, gradually mixing in the dry ingredients to make a smooth batter. Divide the cake batter among the prepared pans.

Bake in the preheated oven for 35–45 minutes, or until springy to the touch. Let cool in the pans for 5 minutes, then turn out onto a wire rack to cool completely.

For the filling, dissolve the instant coffee in the boiling water and place in a bowl with the cream and confectioners' sugar. Whip until the cream is just holding its shape. Use half of the cream to sandwich the 3 cakes together. Spread the remaining cream over the top and sides of the cake. Lightly press the grated chocolate into the cream around the edge of the cake.

Transfer to a serving plate. Lay the caraque over the top of the cake. Cut a few thin strips of waxed paper and place on top of the caraque. Dust lightly with confectioners' sugar, then carefully remove the paper. Serve.

unsalted butter, for greasing

1¾ cups self-rising flour

¼ tsp baking powder

4 tbsp unsweetened cocoa

½ cup superfine sugar

2 eggs

2 tbsp corn syrup

⅔ cup sunflower oil

⅔ cup milk

FILLING

1 tsp instant coffee powder

1 tbsp boiling water

1¼ cups heavy cream

2 tbsp confectioners' sugar

TO DECORATE

1¾ oz/50 g chocolate, grated

marbled chocolate caraque

confectioners' sugar, for dusting

Almond & Hazelnut Gâteau

SERVES 8

Preheat the oven to 375°F/190°C. Grease two 7-inch/18-cm layer cake pans and line with parchment paper.

Whisk the eggs and superfine sugar in a large mixing bowl with an electric mixer for about 10 minutes, or until the mixture is very light and foamy and a trail is left when the whisk is dragged across the surface.

Fold in the ground nuts, then sift the flour and fold in with a metal spoon or spatula. Pour into the prepared pans.

Scatter the slivered almonds over the top of one of the cakes. Bake both of the cakes in the preheated oven for 15–20 minutes, or until springy to the touch.

Let cool slightly in the pans. Carefully remove the cakes from the pans and transfer to a wire rack to cool completely.

Meanwhile, make the filling. Melt the chocolate in a heatproof bowl set over a saucepan of gently simmering water. Remove from the heat, and stir in the butter. Let the mixture cool slightly. Whip the cream until just holding its shape, then fold in the melted chocolate until mixed.

Place the cake without the extra almonds on a serving plate and spread the filling over it. Let the filling set slightly, then place the almond-topped cake on top and chill for about 1 hour. Dust with confectioners' sugar and serve.

unsalted butter, for greasing
4 eggs
1/2 cup superfine sugar
1/2 cup ground almonds
1/2 cup ground hazelnuts
1/3 cup all-purpose flour
1/2 cup slivered almonds

FILLING
3 1/2 oz/100 g semisweet
  chocolate
1 tbsp unsalted butter
1 1/4 cups heavy cream
confectioners' sugar, for dusting

Mississippi Mud Pie

SERVES 8

To make the pie dough, sift the flour and cocoa into a mixing bowl. Rub in the butter with your fingertips until the mixture resembles fine bread crumbs. Stir in the sugar and enough cold water to mix to a soft dough. Wrap the dough in plastic wrap and let chill in the refrigerator for 15 minutes.

Preheat the oven to 375°F/190°C. Roll out the dough on a lightly floured counter and use to line a 9-inch/23-cm loose-bottom tart pan or ceramic pie dish. Line with parchment paper and fill with dried beans or baking beans. Bake in the oven for 15 minutes. Remove from the oven and take out the paper and beans. Bake the pie shell for an additional 10 minutes.

To make the filling, beat the butter and sugar together in a bowl and gradually beat in the eggs with the cocoa. Melt the chocolate in a heatproof bowl set over a saucepan of gently simmering water, then beat it into the mixture with the light cream and the chocolate extract.

Reduce the oven temperature to 325°F/160°C. Pour the mixture into the pie shell and bake for 45 minutes, or until the filling has set gently.

Let the mud pie cool completely, then transfer it to a serving plate. Cover with the whipped cream.

Decorate the pie with chocolate flakes and curls and then let chill until ready to serve.

PIE DOUGH

1 1/2 cups all-purpose flour, plus extra for dusting
2 tbsp unsweetened cocoa
generous 1/2 cup unsalted butter
2 tbsp superfine sugar
1–2 tbsp cold water

FILLING

3/4 cup unsalted butter
scant 1 3/4 cups packed brown sugar
4 eggs, lightly beaten
4 tbsp unsweetened cocoa, sifted
5 1/2 oz/150 g semisweet chocolate, broken into pieces
1 1/4 cups light cream
1 tsp chocolate extract

TO DECORATE

scant 2 cups heavy cream, whipped
chocolate flakes and curls

Blackberry Chocolate Flan

SERVES 6

To make the pie dough, sift the flour, cocoa, confectioners' sugar, and salt into a mixing bowl and make a well in the center. Place the butter and egg yolk in the well and gradually mix in the dry ingredients, using a dough mixer or two forks. Knead lightly and form into a ball. Wrap the pie dough in plastic wrap and let chill in the refrigerator for 1 hour.

Preheat the oven to 350°F/180°C. Roll out the dough on a lightly floured counter. Use it to line a 12 x 4-inch/30 x 10-cm rectangular flan pan and prick the pie shell with a fork. Line the bottom with parchment paper and fill with dried beans or baking beans. Bake in the preheated oven for 15 minutes. Remove the flan pan from the oven, remove the paper and beans, and set aside to cool.

To make the filling, place the cream and jelly in a saucepan and bring to a boil over low heat. Remove from the heat and stir in the chocolate and then the butter until melted and smooth. Pour the mixture into the pie shell and set aside to cool.

To make the sauce, put the blackberries, lemon juice, and superfine sugar in a food processor and process until smooth. Strain through a nylon sieve into a bowl and stir in the cassis. Set aside.

Remove the flan from the pan and place on a serving plate. Arrange the remaining blackberries on top and brush with a little blackberry and liqueur sauce. Serve the flan with the remaining sauce on the side.

PIE DOUGH

1 cup all-purpose flour, plus extra for dusting

1/4 cup unsweetened cocoa

1/2 cup confectioners' sugar

pinch of salt

6 tbsp unsalted butter, cut into small pieces

1/2 egg yolk

FILLING

1 1/4 cups heavy cream

6 oz/175 g blackberry jelly

8 oz/225 g semisweet chocolate, broken into pieces

2 tbsp unsalted butter, cut into small pieces

SAUCE

1 lb 8 oz/675 g blackberries, plus extra for decoration

1 tbsp lemon juice

2 tbsp superfine sugar

2 tbsp crème de cassis

Chocolate Mousse Tart

SERVES 8

To make the tart shell, mix the graham crackers and amaretti cookies with the butter and press well into the bottom of a 9-inch/23-cm springform cake pan. Chill in the refrigerator.

For the topping, melt the semisweet and milk chocolate in a heatproof bowl set over a saucepan of gently simmering water. Cool slightly, then add the egg yolks and mix well.

In a separate bowl, whip the egg whites until they form soft peaks, then add the superfine sugar and whip until stiff.

Fold the chocolate mixture into the egg whites and pour over the tart shell. Chill in the refrigerator for 8 hours or overnight.

When you are ready to serve the tart, unmold it, transfer to a serving dish, and crumble the chocolate flake bars over the top.

3 oz/85 g graham crackers, crushed

3 oz/85 g amaretti cookies, crushed

5 tbsp unsalted butter, melted

TOPPING

7 oz/200 g semisweet chocolate, broken into pieces

4 oz/115 g milk chocolate, broken into pieces

3 large eggs, separated

1/4 cup superfine sugar

3 chocolate flake bars, to decorate

Coffee-Time Treats

Double Chocolate Muffins

MAKES 12

Preheat the oven to 400°F/200°C. Line a 12-cup muffin pan with paper liners. Sift the flour, cocoa, baking powder, and cinnamon into a large mixing bowl. Stir in the sugar and 4^1/2 oz/125 g of the white chocolate.

Place the eggs and oil in a separate bowl and whisk until frothy, then gradually whisk in the milk. Stir into the dry ingredients until just blended. Divide the batter evenly among the paper liners, filling each three-quarters full. Bake in the oven for 20 minutes, or until well risen and springy to the touch. Remove the muffins from the oven, let cool in the pan for 2 minutes, then remove and place them on a cooling rack to cool completely.

Place the remaining white chocolate in a heatproof bowl, set the bowl over a saucepan of barely simmering water, and heat until melted. Spread over the top of the muffins. Let set, then dust the tops with a little cocoa and serve.

scant 1^1/2 cups all-purpose flour
^{1}/3 cup unsweetened cocoa, plus extra for dusting
1 tbsp baking powder
1 tsp ground cinnamon
^{1}/2 cup superfine sugar
6^1/2 oz/185 g white chocolate, broken into pieces
2 large eggs
^{1}/3 cup sunflower oil or peanut oil
1 cup milk

Chocolate Orange Muffins

MAKES 8–10

Preheat the oven to 375°F/190°C. Thoroughly oil 10 cups of a 12-cup muffin pan.

Sift both flours into a mixing bowl and stir in the ground almonds and sugar.

Mix the orange zest and juice, cream cheese, and eggs together in a separate bowl. Make a well in the center of the dry ingredients and stir in the wet ingredients, then add the chocolate chips. Beat well to combine all the ingredients.

Divide the batter evenly among the cups, filling each no more than three-quarters full.

Bake in the oven for 20–25 minutes until well risen and golden brown.

Remove from the oven and let cool slightly on a cooling rack, but eat them as fresh as possible.

sunflower oil or peanut oil,
   for oiling
scant 1 cup self-rising white flour
scant 1 cup self-rising whole
   wheat flour
1/4 cup ground almonds
1/4 cup packed brown sugar
zest and juice of 1 orange
3/4 cup cream cheese
2 large eggs
1/3 cup semisweet chocolate chips

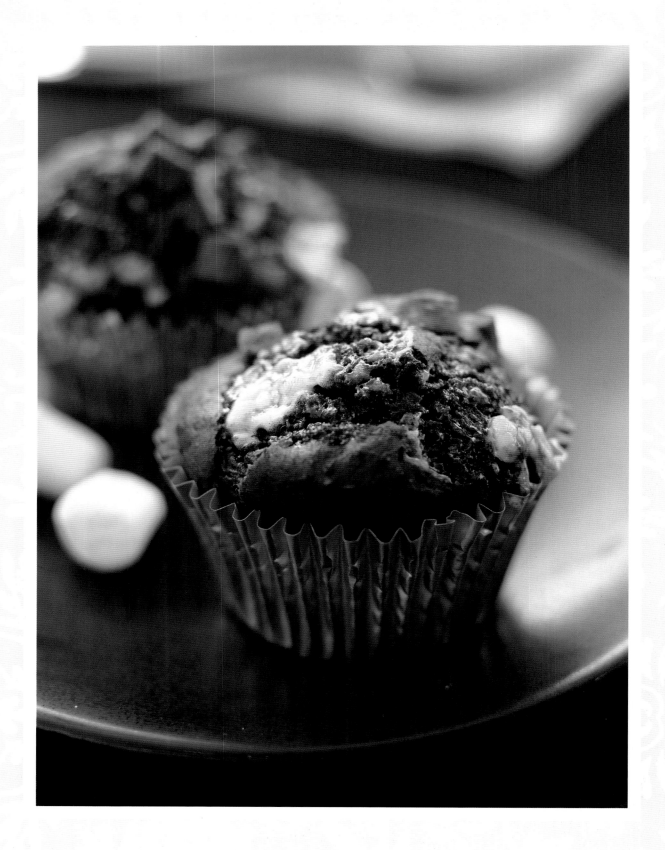

Marshmallow Muffins

MAKES 12

Preheat the oven to 375°F/190°C. Line a 12-cup muffin pan with paper liners. Melt the butter in a saucepan.

Sift the flour, cocoa, and baking powder together in a large bowl. Stir in the sugar, chocolate chips, and marshmallows until thoroughly mixed.

Whisk the egg, milk, and melted butter together in a separate bowl, then gently stir into the flour to form a stiff batter. Divide the batter evenly among the paper liners.

Bake in the oven for 20–25 minutes until well risen. Remove from the oven and let cool in the pan for 5 minutes, then place on a cooling rack and let cool completely.

5 tbsp unsalted butter

2 cups all-purpose flour

6 tbsp unsweetened cocoa

3 tsp baking powder

6 tbsp superfine sugar

1/2 cup milk chocolate chips

1/4 cup multicolored mini marshmallows

1 large egg, beaten

1 1/4 cups milk

Double Chocolate Brownies with Fudge Sauce

MAKES 9 LARGE OR 16 SMALL

Preheat the oven to 350°F/180°C. Grease and line a 7-inch/18-cm square cake pan with parchment paper. Place the butter and chocolate in a small heatproof bowl set over a saucepan of gently simmering water until melted. Stir until smooth. Let cool slightly. Stir in the sugar, salt, and vanilla extract. Add the eggs, one at a time, stirring well, until blended.

Sift the flour and unsweetened cocoa into the cake batter and beat until smooth. Stir in the chocolate chips, then pour the batter into the pan. Bake in the preheated oven for 35–40 minutes, or until the top is evenly colored and a skewer inserted into the center comes out almost clean. Let cool slightly while preparing the sauce.

To make the sauce, place the butter, sugar, milk, cream, and corn syrup in a small saucepan and heat gently until the sugar has dissolved. Bring to a boil and stir for 10 minutes, or until the mixture is caramel-color. Remove from the heat and add the chocolate. Stir until smooth. Cut the brownies into large or small squares and serve immediately with the sauce.

½ cup unsalted butter, plus
   extra for greasing
4 oz/115 g semisweet chocolate,
   broken into pieces
1⅓ cups superfine sugar
pinch of salt
1 tsp vanilla extract
2 large eggs
1 cup all-purpose flour
2 tbsp unsweetened cocoa
½ cup white chocolate chips

FUDGE SAUCE
4 tbsp butter
1 cup superfine sugar
⅔ cup milk
1 cup heavy cream
⅔ cup corn syrup
7 oz/200 g semisweet chocolate,
   broken into pieces

Black Russian Brownies

MAKES 8–10

Preheat the oven to 350°F/180°C. Grease and line a 12 x 8-inch/30 x 20-cm shallow cake pan with parchment paper.

Melt the chocolate and the butter with the peppercorns in a small saucepan over low heat. Remove from the heat and let cool slightly.

Beat together the eggs, sugar, and vanilla extract in a large bowl and stir in the chocolate mixture, Kahlúa, and vodka.

Sift the flour and baking powder into a separate bowl, then stir evenly into the chocolate mixture. Stir in the walnuts. Pour into the pan and bake for 20–25 minutes, until just firm to the touch.

Let cool for a few minutes, then cut into bars or squares and lift carefully from the pan onto serving plates.

For the topping, stir the Kahlúa into the crème fraîche and spoon a generous mound on each serving of brownie. Dust with a little unsweetened cocoa and serve immediately.

$\frac{1}{2}$ cup unsalted butter, plus
  extra for greasing
4 oz/115 g bittersweet chocolate,
  broken into pieces
$\frac{1}{2}$ tsp coarsely ground black
  peppercorns
4 eggs, beaten
$1\frac{1}{4}$ cups superfine sugar
1 tsp vanilla extract
3 tbsp Kahlúa liqueur
2 tbsp vodka
$1\frac{1}{3}$ cups all-purpose flour
$\frac{1}{4}$ tsp baking powder
$\frac{1}{2}$ cup chopped walnuts

KAHLUA CREAM TOPPING
2 tbsp Kahlúa liqueur
scant 1 cup crème fraîche or
  sour cream
unsweetened cocoa, for dusting

Chocolate Butterfly Cakes

MAKES 12

Preheat the oven to 350°F/180°C. Put 12 paper liners in a muffin pan, or put 12 double-layer paper liners on a cookie sheet.

Put the margarine, sugar, flour, eggs, and cocoa in a large bowl and, using a handheld electric mixer, beat together until just smooth. Beat in the melted chocolate. Spoon the batter into the paper cases, filling them three-quarters full.

Bake the cupcakes in the preheated oven for 15 minutes, or until springy to the touch. Transfer to a wire rack and let cool.

To make the filling, put the butter in a bowl and beat until fluffy. Sift in the confectioners' sugar and beat together until smooth. Add the melted chocolate and beat together until well mixed.

When the cupcakes are cooled, use a serrated knife to cut a circle from the top of each cake and then cut each circle in half. Spread or pipe a little of the buttercream into the center of each cupcake and press the 2 semicircular halves into it at an angle to resemble butterfly wings. Dust with sifted confectioners' sugar before serving.

1/2 cup soft margarine
1/2 cup superfine sugar
1 1/2 cups self-rising white flour
2 large eggs
2 tbsp unsweetened cocoa
1 oz/25 g semisweet chocolate, melted
confectioners' sugar, for dusting

filling
6 tbsp unsalted butter, softened
1 1/2 cups confectioners' sugar
1 oz/25 g semisweet chocolate, melted

Dark & White Fudge Cupcakes

MAKES 20

Preheat the oven to 350°F/180°C. Put 20 paper liners in 2 muffin pans, or put 20 double-layer paper cases on 2 cookie sheets.

Put the water, butter, superfine sugar, and corn syrup in a saucepan. Heat gently, stirring, until the sugar has dissolved, then bring to a boil. Reduce the heat and cook gently for 5 minutes. Remove from the heat and let cool.

Meanwhile, put the milk and vanilla extract in a bowl. Add the baking soda and stir to dissolve. Sift the flour and cocoa into a separate bowl and add the corn syrup mixture. Stir in the milk and beat until smooth. Spoon the batter into the paper cases until they are two-thirds full.

Bake the cupcakes in the preheated oven for 20 minutes, or until well risen and firm to the touch. Transfer to a wire rack and let cool.

To make the frosting, break the semisweet chocolate into a small heatproof bowl, add half the water and half the butter, and set the bowl over a pan of gently simmering water until melted. Stir until smooth and let stand over the water. Using another bowl, repeat with the white chocolate and remaining water and butter. Sift half the sugar into each bowl and beat until smooth and thick. Top the cupcakes with the frostings. Let set. Serve decorated with chocolate shavings.

scant 1 cup water

6 tbsp unsalted butter

6 tbsp superfine sugar

1 tbsp corn syrup

3 tbsp milk

1 tsp vanilla extract

1 tsp baking soda

1½ cups all-purpose flour

2 tbsp unsweetened cocoa

FROSTING

1¾ oz/50 g semisweet chocolate

4 tbsp water

3½ tbsp unsalted butter

1¾ oz/50 g white chocolate

3 cups confectioners' sugar

CHOCOLATE SHAVINGS

3½ oz/100 g semisweet
   chocolate

3½ oz/100 g white chocolate

Warm Molten-Centered Chocolate Cupcakes

MAKES 8

Preheat the oven to 375°F/190°C. Put 8 paper liners in a muffin pan, or put 8 double-layer paper cases on a cookie sheet.

Put the margarine, sugar, egg, flour, and cocoa in a large bowl and, using a handheld electric mixer, beat together until just smooth.

Spoon half of the batter into the paper cases. Using a teaspoon, make an indentation in the center of each cake. Break the chocolate evenly into 8 squares and place a piece in each indentation, then spoon the remaining cake batter on top.

Bake the cupcakes in the preheated oven for 20 minutes, or until well risen and springy to the touch. Leave the cupcakes for 2–3 minutes before serving warm, dusted with sifted confectioners' sugar.

4 tbsp soft margarine
1/4 cup superfine sugar
1 large egg
1/2 cup self-rising flour
1 tbsp unsweetened cocoa
2 oz/55 g semisweet chocolate
confectioners' sugar, for dusting

Mocha Cupcakes with Whipped Cream

MAKES 20

Preheat the oven to 350°F/180°C. Put 20 paper liners in 2 muffin pans, or put 20 double-layer paper cases on 2 cookie sheets.

Put the coffee powder, butter, sugar, honey, and water in a saucepan and heat gently, stirring, until the sugar has dissolved. Bring to a boil, then reduce the heat and let simmer for 5 minutes. Pour into a large heatproof bowl and let cool.

When the mixture has cooled, sift in the flour and cocoa. Dissolve the baking soda in the milk, then add to the mixture with the egg and beat together until smooth. Spoon the batter into the paper cases.

Bake the cupcakes in the preheated oven for 15–20 minutes, or until well risen and firm to the touch. Transfer to a wire rack to cool.

For the topping, whip the cream in a bowl until it holds its shape. Just before serving, spoon heaping teaspoonfuls of cream on top of each cake, then dust lightly with sifted cocoa. Store the cupcakes in the refrigerator until ready to serve.

2 tbsp instant espresso coffee powder
6 tbsp unsalted butter
6 tbsp superfine sugar
1 tbsp honey
scant 1 cup water
1½ cups all-purpose flour
2 tbsp unsweetened cocoa
1 tsp baking soda
3 tbsp milk
1 large egg, lightly beaten

TOPPING
1 cup whipping cream
unsweetened cocoa, sifted, for dusting

Tiny Chocolate Cupcakes with Ganache Frosting

MAKES 20

Preheat the oven to 375°F/190°C. Put 20 double-layer mini paper liners on 2 cookie sheets.

Put the butter and sugar in a bowl and beat together until light and fluffy. Gradually beat in the egg. Sift in the flour and cocoa and then, using a metal spoon, fold them into the mixture. Stir in the milk.

Take a pastry bag fitted with a large plain tip, fill it with the batter, and pipe it into the paper cases, filling each one half full.

Bake the cakes in the preheated oven for 10–15 minutes, or until well risen and firm to the touch. Transfer to a wire rack to cool.

To make the frosting, break the chocolate into a pan and add the cream. Heat gently, stirring all the time, until the chocolate has melted. Pour into a large heatproof bowl and, using a handheld electric mixer, beat the mixture for 10 minutes, or until thick, glossy, and cool.

Take a pastry bag fitted with a large star tip, fill it with the frosting, and pipe a swirl on top of each cupcake. Alternatively, spoon the frosting over the top of each cupcake. Chill in the refrigerator for 1 hour before serving. Serve decorated with a chocolate-coated coffee bean (if using).

4 tbsp unsalted butter, softened

$\frac{1}{4}$ cup superfine sugar

1 large egg, lightly beaten

scant $\frac{1}{2}$ cup white self-rising flour

2 tbsp unsweetened cocoa

1 tbsp milk

20 chocolate-coated coffee beans, to decorate (optional)

FROSTING

$3\frac{1}{2}$ oz/100 g semisweet chocolate

$\frac{1}{3}$ cup heavy cream

Crumbly Chocolate

Chocolate Chip Oatmeal Cookies

MAKES 20

Preheat the oven to 350°F/180°C. Grease 2 large cookie sheets. Place the butter and sugar in a bowl and beat together with a wooden spoon until light and fluffy.

Beat in the egg, then add the rolled oats, milk, and vanilla extract. Beat together until well blended. Sift the flour, cocoa, and baking powder together and stir into the mixture. Stir in the chocolate pieces.

Place dessertspoonfuls of the mixture on the prepared cookie sheets and flatten slightly with a fork. Bake in the preheated oven for 15 minutes, or until slightly risen and firm. Remove from the oven and cool on the cookie sheets for 2 minutes, then transfer to cooling racks to cool completely.

½ cup unsalted butter, softened, plus extra for greasing
½ cup light brown sugar
1 egg
⅔ cup rolled oats
1 tbsp milk
1 tsp vanilla extract
scant 1 cup all-purpose flour
1 tbsp unsweetened cocoa
½ tsp baking powder
6 squares bittersweet chocolate, broken into pieces
6 squares milk chocolate, broken into pieces

Black & White Cookies

MAKES 18–20

Melt the bittersweet chocolate in a heatproof bowl set over a saucepan of gently simmering water. Remove from the heat and let cool. Sift the flour and baking powder together.

Meanwhile, in a large bowl, whisk the egg, sugar, oil, and vanilla extract together. Whisk in the cooled, melted chocolate until well blended, then gradually stir in the flour. Cover the bowl with plastic wrap and chill in the refrigerator for at least 3 hours.

Preheat the oven to 375°F/190°C. Oil 1 or 2 large cookie sheets. Shape tablespoonfuls of the mixture into log shapes using your hands, each measuring about 2 inches/5 cm. Roll the logs generously in the confectioners' sugar, then place on the prepared cookie sheets, allowing room for the cookies to spread during cooking.

Bake the cookies in the preheated oven for 15 minutes, or until firm. Remove from the oven, and place 3 chocolate buttons down the center of each, alternating the colors. Transfer to a cooling rack and let cool.

2 squares bittersweet chocolate, broken into pieces
1 cup all-purpose flour
1 tsp baking powder
1 egg
scant ¾ cup superfine sugar
scant ¼ cup corn oil, plus extra for oiling
½ tsp vanilla extract
2 tbsp confectioners' sugar
1 small package milk chocolate buttons (about 30 buttons)
1 small package white chocolate buttons (about 30 buttons)

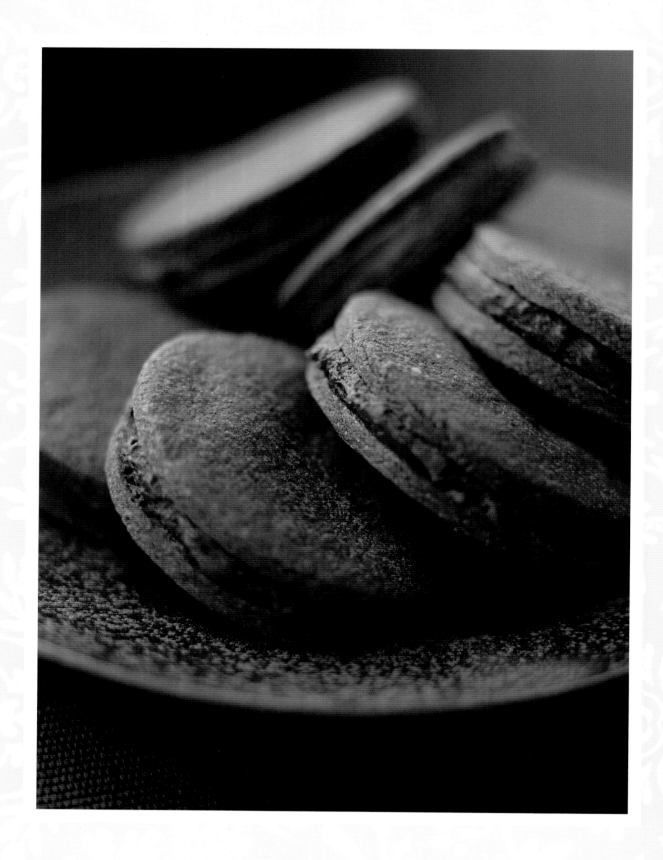

Cookies & Cream Sandwiches

SERVES 4

Preheat the oven to 325°F/160°C. Line a cookie sheet with parchment paper. Place the butter and sugar in a large bowl and beat together until light and fluffy. Sift the flour, unsweetened cocoa, and ground cinnamon into the bowl and mix to form a dough.

Place the dough between 2 sheets of parchment paper and roll out to $^1/_8$ inch/ 3 mm thick. Cut out $2^1/_2$-inch/6-cm circles and place on the prepared cookie sheet. Bake in the oven for 15 minutes or until firm to the touch. Let cool for 2 minutes, then transfer to wire racks to cool completely.

Meanwhile, make the filling. Place the chocolate and cream in a pan and heat gently until the chocolate has melted. Stir until smooth. Let cool, then let chill in the refrigerator for 2 hours, or until firm. Sandwich the cookies together in pairs, each with a spoonful of chocolate cream, and serve dusted with the cocoa.

generous $^1/_2$ cup unsalted
   butter, softened
scant $^3/_4$ cup confectioners'
   sugar
scant 1 cup all-purpose flour
6 tbsp unsweetened cocoa, plus
   extra for dusting
$^1/_2$ tsp ground cinnamon

FILLING
$4^1/_2$ oz/125 g semisweet
   chocolate, broken into pieces
$^1/_4$ cup heavy cream

White Chocolate Cookies

MAKES 24

Preheat the oven to 375°F/190°C. Grease several cookie sheets lightly with a little butter. In a large mixing bowl, cream together the butter and sugar until light and fluffy.

Gradually add the beaten egg to the creamed mixture, beating well after each addition.

Sift the flour and salt into the creamed mixture and blend well.

Stir in the white chocolate chunks and the chopped Brazil nuts.

Place heaping teaspoonfuls of the dough on the prepared cookie sheets. Put no more than 6 on each sheet because the cookies will spread during cooking.

Bake in the oven for 10–12 minutes, or until just golden brown.

Transfer the cookies to wire racks and let stand until completely cooled.

$\frac{1}{2}$ cup unsalted butter, softened, plus extra for greasing

$\frac{2}{3}$ cup brown sugar

1 egg, beaten

$1\frac{3}{4}$ cups self-rising flour

pinch of salt

$4\frac{1}{2}$ oz/125 g white chocolate, chopped

$\frac{1}{3}$ cup chopped Brazil nuts

Chocolate Peanut Butter Slices

MAKES 26

Preheat the oven to 350°F/180°C. Finely chop the chocolate. Sift the flour and baking powder into a large bowl.

Add the butter to the flour and rub in until the mixture resembles bread crumbs. Stir in the sugar, oats, and chopped nuts.

Put a quarter of the mixture into a bowl and stir in the chopped chocolate. Set aside.

Stir the egg into the remaining mixture, then press into the bottom of a 12 x 8-inch/ 30 x 20-cm roasting pan.

Bake the bottom layer in the preheated oven for 15 minutes. Meanwhile, mix the condensed milk and peanut butter together. Pour the mixture over the bottom layer and spread evenly, then sprinkle the reserved chocolate mixture on top and press down lightly.

Return to the oven and bake for an additional 20 minutes, until golden brown. Let cool in the pan, then cut into slices.

10½ oz/300 g milk chocolate

2½ cups all-purpose flour

1 tsp baking powder

1 cup unsalted butter

1¾ cups brown sugar

2 cups rolled oats

½ cup chopped mixed nuts

1 egg, beaten

scant 1¾ cups condensed milk

⅓ cup crunchy peanut butter

Brazil Nut Brittle

MAKES APPROX 20 PIECES

Brush the bottom of an 8-inch/20-cm square cake pan with oil and line with parchment paper. Melt half the semisweet chocolate in a heatproof bowl over a saucepan of gently simmering water and spread in the prepared pan.

Sprinkle with the chopped Brazil nuts, white chocolate, and fudge. Melt the remaining semisweet chocolate pieces and pour over the top.

Let the brittle set, then break up into jagged pieces using the tip of a strong knife.

sunflower oil, for brushing
12 oz/350 g semisweet
   chocolate, broken into pieces
scant ¾ cup chopped Brazil nuts
6 oz/175 g white chocolate,
   coarsely chopped
6 oz/175 g fudge, coarsely
   chopped

Chocolate Pistachio Bars

MAKES 24

Preheat the oven to 325°F/160°C. Grease a cookie sheet with butter. Put the chocolate and butter in a heatproof bowl set over a saucepan of gently simmering water. Stir over low heat until melted and smooth. Remove from the heat and cool slightly.

Sift the flour and baking powder into a bowl and mix in the superfine sugar, cornmeal, lemon zest, amaretto, egg, and pistachios. Stir in the chocolate mixture and mix to a soft dough.

Lightly dust your hands with flour, divide the dough in half, and shape each piece into an 11-inch/28-cm long cylinder. Transfer the cylinders to the prepared cookie sheet and flatten, with the palm of your hand, to about $3/4$ inch/2 cm thick. Bake in the preheated oven for about 20 minutes, until firm to the touch.

Remove the cookie sheet from the oven and let the cooked pieces cool. When cool, put the cooked pieces on a cutting board and slice them diagonally into thin cookies. Return them to the cookie sheet and bake for an additional 10 minutes, until crisp. Remove from the oven, and transfer to a wire rack to cool. Dust lightly with confectioners' sugar.

2 tbsp unsalted butter, plus
  extra for greasing
6 oz/175 g semisweet chocolate,
  broken into pieces
$2^1/_2$ cups self-rising flour, plus
  extra for dusting
$1^1/_2$ tsp baking powder
scant $1/_2$ cup superfine sugar
$1/_2$ cup cornmeal
finely grated zest of 1 lemon
2 tsp amaretto
1 egg, lightly beaten
$3/_4$ cup coarsely chopped
  pistachios
2 tbsp confectioners' sugar,
  for dusting

Chocolate Caramel Squares

MAKES 16

Preheat the oven to 350°F/180°C. Beat together the margarine and brown sugar in a bowl until light and fluffy. Beat in the flour and the rolled oats. Use your fingertips to bring the mixture together, if necessary.

Press the mixture into the bottom of a shallow 8-inch/20-cm square cake pan.

Bake the mixture in the preheated oven for 25 minutes, or until just golden and firm. Cool in the pan.

Place the ingredients for the caramel filling in a saucepan and heat gently, stirring until the sugar has dissolved. Bring slowly to a boil over very low heat, then boil very gently for 3–4 minutes, stirring constantly, until thickened.

Pour the caramel filling over the oat layer in the pan and let set.

For the topping, melt the semisweet chocolate and spread it over the caramel. If using the white chocolate, place it in a heatproof bowl set over a saucepan of gently simmering water until melted. Pipe lines of white chocolate over the semisweet chocolate. Using a toothpick, feather the white chocolate into the semisweet chocolate. Let set, then cut into squares to serve.

1/3 cup soft margarine
1/3 cup brown sugar
1 cup all-purpose flour
1/2 cup rolled oats

CARAMEL FILLING
2 tbsp unsalted butter
2 tbsp brown sugar
3/4 cup condensed milk

TOPPING
3 1/2 oz/100 g semisweet
  chocolate
1 oz/25 g white chocolate
  (optional)

Cookie Sandwiches

MAKES 20

Line 3 cookie sheets with parchment paper, or use 3 nonstick sheets. Cream the butter and sugar together until pale and fluffy. Beat in the egg yolk, then beat in the almonds and flour. Continue beating until thoroughly mixed. Shape the dough into a ball, wrap in plastic wrap, and chill in the refrigerator for $1^1/_2$–2 hours.

Preheat the oven to 325°F/160°C. Unwrap the dough, break off walnut-size pieces, and roll them into balls between the palms of your hands. Place the dough balls on the prepared cookie sheets, allowing space for the cookies to spread during cooking. You may need to cook them in batches. Bake in the preheated oven for 20–25 minutes, until golden. Carefully transfer the cookies, still on the parchment paper (if using), to wire racks to cool.

Melt the chocolate in a heatproof bowl set over a saucepan of gently simmering water. Remove the cookies from the parchment paper (if using). Spread the melted chocolate on the flat sides and sandwich them together in pairs. Return to the wire racks to cool.

2 cup unsalted butter, sweet
  for preference
$1/_2$ cup superfine sugar
1 egg yolk
1 cup ground almonds
$1^1/_4$ cups all-purpose flour
2 oz/55 g semisweet chocolate,
  broken into pieces

Chocolate Liqueurs

MAKES 20

Line a cookie sheet with parchment paper. Break the semisweet chocolate into pieces, place in a bowl and set over a saucepan of hot water. Stir until melted. Spoon the chocolate into 20 paper candy cases, spreading up the sides with a small spoon or brush. Place upside down on the cookie sheet and let set.

Carefully peel away the paper cases. Place a cherry half or nut in the bottom of each cup.

To make the filling, place the heavy cream in a mixing bowl and sift the confectioners' sugar on top. Whip the cream until it is just holding its shape, then whisk in the liqueur to flavor it.

Place the cream in a pastry bag fitted with a 1/2-inch/1-cm plain tip and pipe a little into each chocolate case. Let chill for 20 minutes.

To finish, spoon the semisweet chocolate over the cream to cover it. Add the caraque and let harden.

3 1/2 oz/100 g semisweet
  chocolate
about 5 candied cherries, halved
about 10 hazelnuts or
  macadamia nuts
2/3 cup heavy cream
2 tbsp confectioners' sugar
4 tbsp liqueur

TO FINISH
1 3/4 oz/50 g semisweet
  chocolate, melted
marbled chocolate caraque,
  to decorate

Delectable Desserts

Italian Chocolate Truffles

MAKES 24

Melt the semisweet chocolate with the liqueur in a bowl set over a saucepan of hot water, stirring until well combined.

Add the butter and stir until it has melted. Stir in the confectioners' sugar and the ground almonds.

Let the mixture stand in a cool place until it is firm enough to roll into 24 balls.

Place the grated chocolate on a plate and roll the truffles in the chocolate to coat them.

Place the truffles in paper candy cases and let chill.

6 oz/175 g semisweet chocolate

2 tbsp amaretto liqueur or orange-flavored liqueur

3 tbsp unsalted butter

4 tbsp confectioners' sugar

1/2 cup ground almonds

1 3/4 oz/50 g semisweet chocolate, grated, to decorate

Chocolate Chip Ice Cream with Hot Chocolate Fudge Sauce

SERVES 4–6

Pour the milk into a heavy-bottom saucepan, add the vanilla bean, and bring almost to a boil. Remove from the heat and let infuse for 30 minutes. Meanwhile, chop the chocolate into small pieces and set aside.

Put the sugar and egg yolks in a large bowl and whisk together until pale and the mixture leaves a trail when the whisk is lifted. Remove the vanilla bean from the milk, then slowly add the milk to the sugar mixture, stirring all the time with a wooden spoon. Strain the mixture into the rinsed-out saucepan or a double boiler and cook over low heat for 10–15 minutes, stirring all the time, until the mixture thickens enough to coat the back of the spoon. Do not boil or it will curdle.

Remove the custard from the heat and let cool for at least 1 hour, stirring from time to time to prevent a skin from forming. Meanwhile, whip the cream until it holds its shape. Keep in the refrigerator until ready to use.

If using an ice-cream machine, fold the cold custard into the whipped cream, then churn the mixture in the machine following the manufacturer's instructions. Just before the ice cream freezes, add the chocolate pieces. Alternatively, freeze the custard in a freezerproof container, uncovered, for 1–2 hours, or until it starts to set around the edges. Turn the custard into a bowl and stir with a fork or beat in a food processor until smooth. Fold in the whipped cream and chocolate pieces. Return to the freezer and freeze for an additional 2–3 hours, or until firm. Cover the container with a lid for storing.

Make the chocolate sauce just before you serve the ice cream. Put the chocolate, butter, and milk in a heatproof bowl set over a saucepan of simmering water and heat gently, stirring occasionally, until the chocolate has melted and the sauce is smooth. Transfer the mixture to a heavy-bottom saucepan and stir in the sugar and corn syrup. Heat gently until the sugar has dissolved, then bring to a boil. Boil, without stirring, for 5 minutes. Serve the hot sauce poured over the ice cream.

1¼ cups whole milk

1 vanilla bean

4 oz/115 g milk chocolate

scant ½ cup sugar

3 egg yolks

1¼ cups heavy whipping cream

4½ oz/125 g chocolate chips

CHOCOLATE FUDGE SAUCE

1¾ oz/50 g milk chocolate, broken into pieces

2 tbsp unsalted butter

4 tbsp whole milk

1 cup brown sugar

2 tbsp corn syrup

Chocolate Praline Ice Cream

SERVES 4–6

To prepare the praline, brush a cookie sheet with oil. Put the sugar, water, and nuts in a large heavy-bottom saucepan and heat gently, stirring, until the sugar has dissolved, then let the mixture bubble gently for 6–10 minutes, or until lightly golden brown. Do not stir the mixture while it is bubbling and make sure that it does not burn. As soon as the mixture has turned golden brown, immediately pour it onto the prepared cookie sheet and spread it out evenly. Let cool for 1 hour, or until cooled and hardened. When the praline has hardened, finely crush it in a food processor or place it in a plastic bag and crush with a hammer.

To prepare the ice cream, put the chocolate and milk in a saucepan and heat gently, stirring, until the chocolate has melted and the mixture is smooth. Remove from the heat.

Put the sugar and egg yolks in a large bowl and whisk together until pale and the mixture leaves a trail when the whisk is lifted. Slowly add the milk mixture, stirring all the time with a wooden spoon. Strain the mixture into the rinsed-out saucepan or a double boiler and cook over low heat for 10–15 minutes, stirring all the time, until the mixture thickens enough to coat the back of the spoon. Do not let the mixture boil or it will curdle.

Remove the custard from the heat and let cool for at least 1 hour, stirring from time to time to prevent a skin from forming. Meanwhile, whip the cream until it holds its shape. Keep in the refrigerator until ready to use. If using an ice-cream machine, fold the cold custard into the whipped cream, then churn the mixture in the machine following the manufacturer's instructions. Just before the ice cream freezes, add the praline. Alternatively, freeze the custard in a freezerproof container, uncovered, for 1–2 hours, or until it starts to set around the edges. Turn the custard into a bowl and stir with a fork or beat in a food processor until smooth. Fold in the whipped cream and praline. Return to the freezer and freeze for an additional 2–3 hours, or until firm.

3 oz/85 g semisweet chocolate, broken into pieces
1¼ cups whole milk
scant ½ cup superfine sugar
3 egg yolks
1¼ cups heavy whipping cream

PRALINE

vegetable oil, for oiling
½ cup granulated sugar
2 tbsp water
scant ⅓ cup blanched almonds

Chocolate Ice Cream Roll

SERVES 8

Line a 15x10-inch/38x25-cm jelly roll pan with waxed paper. Grease the bottom and dust with flour. Put the eggs and superfine sugar in a heatproof bowl set over a pan of gently simmering water. Whisk over low heat for 5–10 minutes until the mixture is pale and fluffy. Remove from the heat and continue beating for 10 minutes until the mixture is cool and the whisk leaves a ribbon trail when lifted. Sift the flour and unsweetened cocoa over the surface and gently fold in.

Preheat the oven to 375°F/190°C. Pour the mixture into the prepared pan and spread out evenly with a spatula. Bake in the preheated oven for 15 minutes, until firm to the touch and starting to shrink from the sides of the pan.

Spread out a clean dish towel and cover with a sheet of parchment paper. Lightly dust the parchment paper with confectioners' sugar. Turn out the cake onto the parchment paper and carefully peel off the lining paper. Trim off any crusty edges. Starting from a short side, pick up the cake and the parchment paper and roll them up together. Wrap the dish towel around the rolled cake and place on a wire rack to cool.

Remove the ice cream from the freezer and put it in the refrigerator for 15–20 minutes to soften slightly. Remove the dish towel and unroll the cake. Spread the ice cream evenly over the cake, then roll it up again, this time without the parchment paper. Wrap the cake in foil and place in the freezer. Remove the cake from the freezer about 20 minutes before serving. Unwrap, place on a serving plate, and dust with confectioners' sugar. Arrange the chocolate caraque over the top. Place the cake in the refrigerator until ready to serve.

unsalted butter, for greasing
¾ cup all-purpose flour, plus extra for dusting
4 eggs
½ cup superfine sugar
3 tbsp unsweetened cocoa
confectioners' sugar, for dusting
2½ cups chocolate ice cream
marbled chocolate caraque, to decorate

Chocolate Ice Cream Bombe

SERVES 4

Put a 6^1/$_4$-cup bombe mold into the freezer and turn the freezer to its lowest setting. Place the eggs, egg yolks, and sugar in a heatproof bowl, and beat together until well blended. Put the light cream and chocolate in a saucepan and heat gently until the chocolate has melted, then continue to heat, stirring constantly, until almost boiling. Pour onto the egg mixture, stirring vigorously, then place the bowl over a saucepan of simmering water. Cook, stirring constantly, until the mixture lightly coats the back of the spoon. Strain into another bowl and let cool. Place the heavy cream in a bowl and whisk until slightly thickened, then fold into the cooled chocolate mixture.

Either freeze in an ice-cream maker, following the manufacturer's directions, or pour the mixture into a freezerproof container, cover, and freeze for 2 hours until just frozen. Spoon into a bowl and beat with a fork to break down the ice crystals. Return to the freezer until almost solid. Line the bombe mold with the chocolate ice cream and return to the freezer. Transfer from the freezer to the refrigerator 30 minutes before serving.

To make the white chocolate ice cream, put the chocolate and half the milk in a saucepan and heat gently until the chocolate has just melted. Remove from the heat and stir. Put the sugar and remaining milk in another saucepan and heat gently until the sugar has melted. Set aside to cool, then stir into the cooled white chocolate mixture. Place the cream in a bowl and whisk until slightly thickened, then fold into the chocolate mixture. Spoon into the center of the bombe, cover, and freeze for about 4 hours, until firm. To serve, dip the mold briefly into warm water, then turn out onto a serving plate and decorate with the chocolate shapes.

SEMISWEET CHOCOLATE ICE CREAM
2 eggs
2 egg yolks
^{1}/$_2$ cup superfine sugar
1^1/$_4$ cups light cream
8 oz/225 g semisweet chocolate, chopped
1^1/$_4$ cups heavy cream

WHITE CHOCOLATE ICE CREAM
5 oz/140 g white chocolate, broken into pieces
^{2}/$_3$ cup milk
2 oz/55 g superfine sugar
1^1/$_4$ cups heavy cream
chocolate shapes, to decorate

Tiramisù Layers

MAKES 6

Whip the cream until it just holds its shape. Beat the mascarpone to soften slightly, then fold in the whipped cream. Melt the chocolate in a heatproof bowl set over a saucepan of simmering water, stirring occasionally. Let the chocolate cool slightly, then stir it into the mascarpone and cream.

Mix the hot coffee and sugar in a saucepan and stir until dissolved. Let cool, then add the dark rum. Dip the ladyfingers into the mixture briefly so that they absorb the coffee and rum mixture, but do not become soggy.

Place 3 ladyfingers on each of 6 serving plates.

Spoon a layer of the chocolate, mascarpone, and cream mixture over the ladyfingers.

Place 3 more ladyfingers crosswise on top of the chocolate and mascarpone mixture. Spread another layer of chocolate and mascarpone and place 3 more ladyfingers on top.

Let the Tiramisù chill in the refrigerator for at least 1 hour. Dust with a little unsweetened cocoa just before serving.

²⁄₃ cup heavy cream
1¾ cups mascarpone cheese
10 oz/280 g semisweet chocolate
1¾ cups hot black coffee
¼ cup superfine sugar
6 tbsp dark rum or cognac
54 ladyfingers
unsweetened cocoa, for dusting

Chocolate & Orange Slices

SERVES 8

Lightly grease a 1-lb/450-g terrine or loaf pan and line it with plastic wrap. Put the chocolate in a heatproof bowl set over a saucepan of gently simmering water. Stir over a low heat until melted. Remove from the heat and let cool slightly.

Meanwhile, peel the fruit, removing all traces of pith. Cut the zest into very thin strips. Beat the egg yolks into the chocolate, one at a time, then add most of the zest (reserve the rest for decoration) and all the sour cream and raisins, and beat until thoroughly combined. Spoon the mixture into the prepared pan, cover with plastic wrap, and chill in the refrigerator for 3–4 hours, until set.

To serve, remove the loaf pan from the refrigerator and turn out the chocolate mold. Remove the plastic wrap and cut the mold into slices. Place a slice on each of 8 individual serving plates and add whipped cream to serve. Decorate with the remaining zest.

2 tsp unsalted butter,
  for greasing
14 oz/400 g semisweet
  chocolate, broken into pieces
3 small, loose-skinned citrus
  fruit such as oranges,
  tangerines, or mandarins
4 egg yolks
scant 1 cup sour cream
2 tbsp raisins
$1\frac{1}{4}$ cups whipped cream,
  to serve

Chocolate Hazelnut Parfaits

MAKES 6

Preheat the broiler to medium. Spread out the hazelnuts on a cookie sheet and toast under the broiler for about 5 minutes, shaking the sheet from time to time, until golden all over. Set aside to cool.

Put the chocolate in a heatproof bowl set over a saucepan of gently simmering water. Stir over low heat until melted, then remove from the heat and cool. Put the toasted hazelnuts in a food processor and process until finely ground.

Whip the cream until it is stiff, then fold in the ground hazelnuts and set aside. Add 3 tablespoons of the sugar to the egg yolks and beat for 10 minutes until pale and thick.

Whip the egg whites in a separate bowl until soft peaks form. Whisk in the remaining sugar, a little at a time, until the whites are stiff and glossy. Stir the cooled chocolate into the egg yolk mixture, then fold in the cream and finally, fold in the egg whites. Divide the mixture among 6 freezerproof timbales or molds, cover with plastic wrap, and freeze for at least 8 hours, or overnight, until firm.

Transfer the parfaits to the refrigerator about 10 minutes before serving to soften slightly. Turn out onto individual serving plates, dust the tops lightly with unsweetened cocoa, decorate with mint sprigs, and serve with wafers.

$1\frac{1}{2}$ cups blanched hazelnuts

6 oz/175 g semisweet chocolate, broken into small pieces

$2\frac{1}{2}$ cups heavy cream

$2\frac{1}{2}$ cups confectioners' sugar

3 eggs, separated

1 tbsp unsweetened cocoa, for dusting

6 small fresh mint sprigs, to decorate

wafer cookies, to serve

Real Hot Chocolate

SERVES 1–2

Place the chocolate in a large, heatproof pitcher. Place the milk in a heavy-bottom saucepan and bring to a boil. Pour about one-quarter of the milk onto the chocolate and leave until the chocolate has softened.

Whisk the milk and chocolate mixture until smooth. Return the remaining milk to the heat and return to a boil, then pour onto the chocolate, whisking constantly.

Pour into warmed mugs or cups and top with the chocolate curls. Serve immediately.

1$\frac{1}{2}$ oz/40 g semisweet chocolate, broken into pieces
1$\frac{1}{4}$ cups milk
chocolate curls, to decorate

Chocolate Milk Shakes

MAKES 4

Pour the milk, chocolate syrup, and coffee syrup into a food processor and gently process until blended. Add the ice cream and process to a smooth consistency.

Pour into 4 glasses.

To decorate, spoon the cream into a pastry bag with a large, star-shaped tip. Pipe generous amounts of cream on top of the milk shakes. Sprinkle over the cocoa and serve with straws.

1$\frac{1}{4}$ cups milk
2 tbsp chocolate syrup
2 tbsp coffee syrup
1$\frac{1}{4}$–1$\frac{1}{2}$ pints chocolate ice cream

TO DECORATE
$\frac{2}{3}$ cup heavy cream, whipped
unsweetened cocoa, for dusting

INDEX

almonds
almond & hazelnut gâteau 23
chocolate fudge cake 12
chocolate orange muffins 34
chocolate praline ice cream 81
cookie sandwiches 71
marble cake 17
rippled chocolate gâteau 18

bars & slices
chocolate caramel squares 68
chocolate peanut butter slices 62
chocolate pistachio bars 66
black & white cookies 56
black Russian brownies 40
blackberry chocolate flan 26
Brazil nuts
Brazil nut brittle 65
white chocolate cookies 60
brownies
black Russian brownies 40
double chocolate brownies with fudge sauce 38

cakes
almond & hazelnut gâteau 23
chocolate fudge cake 12
chocolate truffle torte 14
marble cake 17
mocha layer cake 20
rippled chocolate gâteau 18
see also cupcakes
candies
Brazil nut brittle 65
chocolate liqueurs 72
cherries: chocolate liqueurs 72
coffee
chocolate milk shakes 94
chocolate truffle torte 14
marble cake 17
mocha cupcakes with whipped cream 49
mocha layer cake 20
tiramisù layers 87
condensed milk
chocolate caramel squares 68
chocolate peanut butter slices 62
cookies
black & white cookies 56
chocolate chip oatmeal cookies 54
cookie sandwiches 71
cookies & cream sandwiches 59

white chocolate cookies 60
see also bars & slices
corn syrup
chocolate chip ice cream with hot chocolate
fudge sauce 78
chocolate fudge cake 12
dark & white fudge cupcakes 44
double chocolate brownies with fudge sauce 38
mocha layer cake 20
rippled chocolate gâteau 18
cream cheese
chocolate orange muffins 34
tiramisù layers 87
cupcakes
chocolate butterfly cakes 43
dark & white fudge cupcakes 44
mocha cupcakes with whipped cream 49
tiny chocolate cupcakes with ganache
frosting 50
warm molten-centered chocolate cupcakes 46

dark & white fudge cupcakes 44
desserts, cold
chocolate hazelnut parfaits 90
chocolate & orange slices 88
tiramisù layers 87
see also ice cream
desserts, hot: chocolate fondue 76
double chocolate brownies with fudge sauce 38
double chocolate muffins 32
drinks
chocolate milk shakes 94
real hot chocolate 93

flans, pies & tarts
blackberry chocolate flan 26
chocolate mousse tart 29
Mississippi mud pie 24
fruit: chocolate fondue 76

hazelnuts
almond & hazelnut gâteau 23
chocolate hazelnut parfaits 90
chocolate liqueurs 72
honey: mocha cupcakes with whipped cream 49

ice cream
chocolate chip, with hot chocolate fudge
sauce 78

chocolate ice cream bombe 84
chocolate ice cream roll 82
chocolate milk shakes 94
chocolate praline 81

liqueurs
black Russian brownies 40
chocolate liqueurs 72
chocolate pistachio bars 66
chocolate truffle torte 14
tiramisù layers 87

marble cake 17
marshmallows: marshmallow muffins 37
Mississippi mud pie 24
mocha cupcakes with whipped cream 49
mocha layer cake 20
muffins
chocolate orange 34
double chocolate 32
marshmallow 37

nuts
chocolate liqueurs 72
chocolate peanut butter slices 62
chocolate pistachio bars 66
see also almonds; Brazil nuts; hazelnuts;
walnuts

oats
chocolate caramel squares 68
chocolate chip oatmeal cookies 54
chocolate peanut butter slices 62
oranges
chocolate & orange slices 88
chocolate orange muffins 34

raisins: chocolate & orange slices 88
real hot chocolate 93
rippled chocolate gâteau 18

tiny chocolate cupcakes with ganache frosting 50
tiramisù layers 87

walnuts: black Russian brownies 40
warm molten-centered chocolate cupcakes 46
white chocolate cookies 60